For Brautigan Zeus,
and also for Penelope and Willow.

Copyright © 2020 by Jessica Laurel Kane

All rights reserved. No part of this book may be reproduced, transmitted, or stored in an information retrieval system in any form or by any means, graphic, electronic, or mechanical, including photocopying, taping, and recording, without prior written permission from the publisher.

First edition 2020

LCCN: 2020918399
ISBN 978-1-7328682-4-3

Printed in China

This book was typeset in Bookbag and Raski.
The illustrations were created using paper and hot glue,
edited digitally.

Visit the author at www.jessicalaurelkane.com

YMMSBILYA PRESS

Anchors in the Storm

written and illustrated by
Jessica Laurel Kane

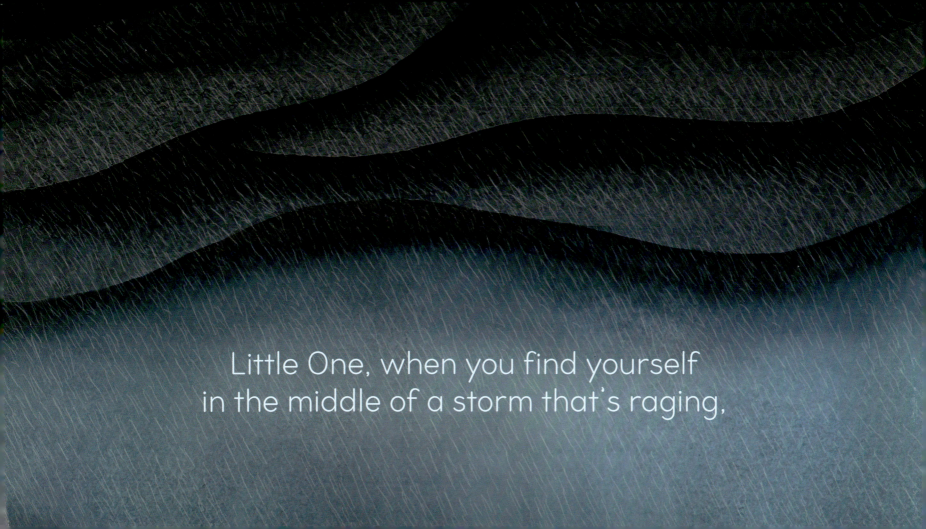
Little One, when you find yourself in the middle of a storm that's raging,

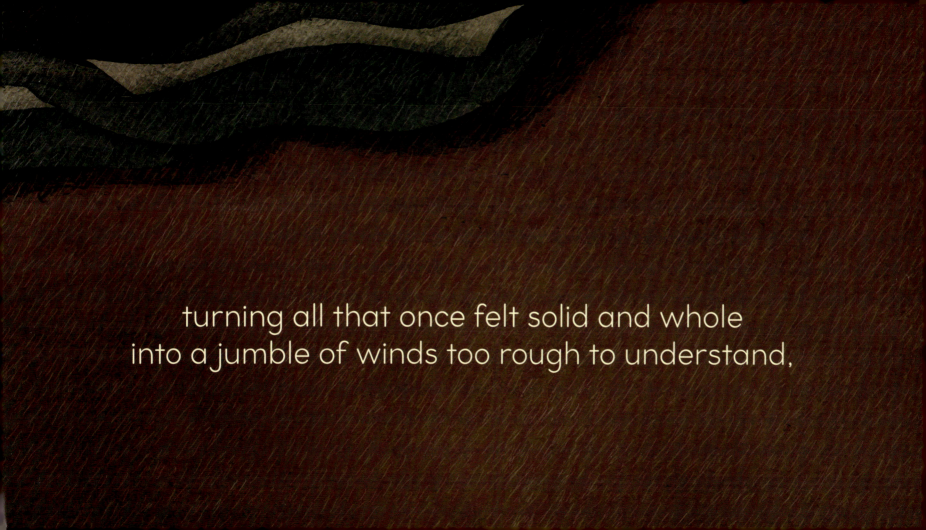

turning all that once felt solid and whole
into a jumble of winds too rough to understand,

amidst your tears and fears and anguish, there is an anchor to keep you steady.

A connection that's here,
right in the middle of all the whirling chaos
that's happening right now.

Find a hand. Hold it. It will hold yours.
Feel the strength. The connection and love.
Strong enough to withstand any weather.

Even when you're scared or worried
because the world feels too different or unfamiliar,
you can rely on your anchor.

Any hand will do. Even your own.

And if you're afraid that someone dear to you is without an anchor in a storm of their own, reach out. Reach out your hand with your words, Little One, just as I'm reaching out to you.

Please believe me: your connection is still here. You may need to anchor deep inside your heart, beneath the sadness, but you will feel that the connection is real, even in the midst of such uncertainty.

The winds will settle, Little One.
The sun will shine. Flowers will bloom.
And yes, storms again will pass through.

But your anchors, your connections,
are always here to stay.